Living Your Best Life

according to

nala cat

Penguin Books

PENGUIN

An imprint of Penguin Random House LLC

First published in the United States of America by Penguin Books,
an imprint of Penguin Random House LLC, 2020

Visit us online at penguinrandomhouse.com

LIBRARY OF CONGRESS CATALOGING-IN-PUBLICATION DATA
Names: Nala (Cat)
Title: Living Your Best Life / According to Nala Cat
Description: [New York]: Penguin Books, 2020. | Audience: Ages 12 Up
Audience: Grades 7–9 | Summary: "A charming guide on how to live your best life
inspired by Instagram's most popular cat"—provided by publisher.
Identifiers: LCCN 2019030327 | ISBN 9780593115046 | ISBN 9780593115268
(ebook) | ISBN 9780593115275 (kindle edition)
Subjects: LCSH: Conduct of Life—Juvenile Humor. | Cats—Juvenile Humor
Classification: LCC PN6231.C6142 N35 2020 | DDC 818/.602—DC23
LC Record available at https://lccn.loc.gov/2019030327

Manufactured in China
1 3 5 7 9 10 8 6 4 2

DEDICATION:

To Jennifer Conrad, veterinarian and founder of the
Paw Project, for her unwavering humanity.

MEOW,
my name is **Nala**.

You might have seen me on social media—I hold the Guinness World Record for being the most popular cat on Instagram. I have plenty of fans—I am pretty cute . . . I was not always the star I am today though.

Up until I was five months old, I lived in a shelter. I was not as fluffy as I am now, and I was sad. But then I was rescued and my entire life changed. My mom saw me at the shelter and reached out to pet me. I licked her hand to let her know I belonged with her. Luckily, Mom felt the same way too.

Now I have a forever family. Adoption and rescuing have always been important to my moms and I. I have other adopted kitty siblings, a pup, and I even have two adopted human sisters! As a former shelter cat, I do everything I can to help other kitties find their forever homes too.

In 2012, my mom started an Instagram account for me. The photos of my cute face went viral across the internet, and people started to say how much they loved me! My followers are my community, and I consider them part of my family.

Every day I strive to make my family smile, laugh, and most of all, feel loved. I aspire to be happy and to spread happiness. I hope this book will encourage you to dream big dreams, love passionately, and live your best life!

Love,
nala cat

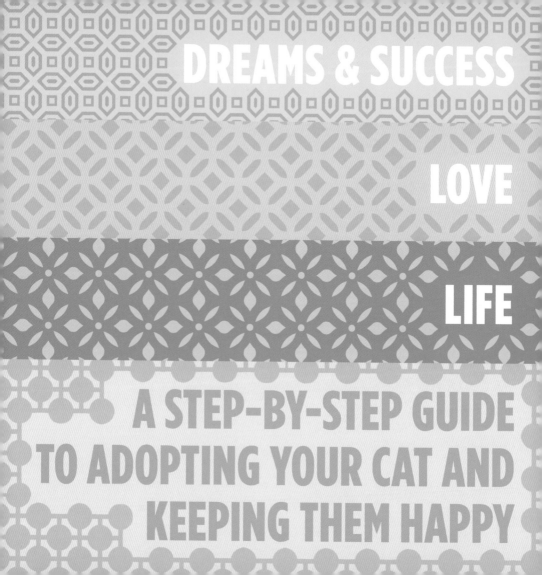

DREAMS & SUCCESS

LOVE

LIFE

A STEP-BY-STEP GUIDE
TO ADOPTING YOUR CAT AND
KEEPING THEM HAPPY

*Are you ready
to live your*

BEST LIFE?

DREAMS & SUCCESS

Sometimes you have
to tell yourself

"I AM A SHARK"

and attack the day.

KEEP YOUR EYES
ON THE PRIZE.

YOU CAN DO IT.

Don't give up!

You're almost there.

Reach your goals

ONE PAW AT A TIME.

If you want something,

CLAW FOR IT.

Let them hear you

~~ROAR.~~
MEOW.

READY.

SET.

SUCCEED.

#workhard

#playhard

Embrace

the

impossible.

Do what makes

YOU HAPPY.

BELIEVE *in yourself.*

You are **AMAZING.**

ANY DAY

is a

GOOD DAY

to start a

NEW DREAM.

It's hard work being

SUCCESSFUL.

GUINNESS
WORLD RECORDS

CERTIFICATE

Nala Cat (USA)
is the most popular cat
on Instagram
with 3.4 million followers
as of 3 May 2017

OFFICIALLY AMAZING

RECORD HOLDER

BE FEARLESS

every step of the way.

Don't let anyone dull your

SPARKLE.

Aim for the sky.

Reach for the stars.

#limitless

LOVE

EMBRACE
your inner hero.

Choose

LOVE.

Choose

YOU.

#selflove

Talking to your

BEST FRIEND

is the

BEST THERAPY.

PAMPER YOURSELF.
Have tuna in bed.

You are

PERFECT

just the way

YOU ARE.

CONFIDENCE

*never goes
out of style.*

#ownit
#workit

Be a
QUEEN.

#flawless
#shinebright

LOVE

is being in your

HAPPY PLACE.

You are
MAGIC!

Be confident,

strong,

happy.

BE YOURSELF.

You are a

GIFT

to the

WORLD.

LIVE

a little more.

LAUGH

a little more.

LOVE

a little more.

Create your own
SUNSHINE.

#choosehappiness

SMILE,
confidence looks
BEAUTIFUL
on you.

Hey girl, you deserve
THE WORLD.

LIFE

SING

like no one is

LISTENING.

Spread

HAPPINESS.

Live life

COURAGEOUSLY.

DAILY REMINDER:

YOU ARE AMAZING.

YOU ARE STRONG.

YOU ARE WORTH IT.

CREATE YOUR OWN CALM.

Be fabulous,
ALWAYS.

A little

SILLINESS

is good for the

SOUL.

Balance is
KEY.

Let your crazy

SHINE.

#beoutrageous

Excuse me,

DID YOU SMILE TODAY?

There's

ALWAYS

time for a

SELFIE.

Everyone needs

ME TIME.

Learn something new

EVERY DAY.

#feedyoursoul

naps =
HAPPINESS

Celebrate

YOURSELF!

ACKNOWLEDGMENTS

First, I would like to thank my editor, Gianna Lakenauth, for her guidance and for helping me become the literary cat that I've always aspired to be. I would like to thank Eileen Kreit, Ken Wright, Maria Fazio (my brilliant designer!), and the entire Penguin Young Readers team for all of their hard work and support. Thank you to Max Brabant, and to Megan Dacus and Lisa Scarsi for your photography contributions. Thank you to my friends, family, and community for supporting me and encouraging me to share my inspiration with the world. Last but not least, thank you to my fans for loving me. I am filled with gratitude for all of you every day!

Love,
nala cat 🐾

A STEP-BY-STEP GUIDE TO ADOPTING YOUR CAT AND KEEPING THEM HAPPY

COMMITMENT

Cats are cute, but they also come with plenty of financial costs. There are the basic necessities such as food, water, and veterinary care, as well as lifestyle necessities such as toys, pet beds, cat trees, etc. These costs can increase as your cat ages, in addition to the amount of care you need to provide.

Once you're ready for the long-term responsibility and financial commitment, it's time to . . .

PREPARE YOUR HOME

Are you renting your house or apartment? First, you should check your rental agreement to know if your rental is pet friendly. Once in the clear, you should store all household cleaners, medicines, and other potentially dangerous substances where your cat can't reach them. It is recommended to replace or get rid of live plants bcause many plants are toxic to cats. You can check ASPCA.org to find out if your plant is toxic or not. Also, put away small objects, strings, and rubber bands, all of which can be very dangerous if swallowed.

PROTECTION

Before bringing your cat home, you should consider microchips, spaying or neutering, and vaccinations. Microchipping your cat is a smart safety measure that increases your chance of reuniting with your cat if they get lost. It is advised to always spay or neuter your cat to prevent unwanted pregnancies. This will prevent overpopulation and help your cat to live a longer, healthier life. You should also make sure your cat receives the vaccines they need, which will depend on if they are an indoor or outdoor cat.

CARING FOR YOUR CAT

Daily ongoing care is essential to have a happy and healthy cat. Here are a few things to consider:

🐾 Grooming: Cats clean themselves and most don't require baths. If you feel like your cat might need a bath, consult your veterinarian. Waterless cat shampoos and pet wipes are great alternatives. A cat's oral hygiene is just as important as yours! They do not like getting their teeth brushed, but try your best. You can schedule a dental appointment with your vet if necessary.

🐾 Food: If you want a happy cat, feed them healthy meals at the same time every day. When shopping for food, avoid purchasing food with grains, artificial coloring, artificial flavoring, and meat by-product meal. Cats need to have access to fresh water and often don't drink enough water. You should have bowls of fresh water throughout your home to encourage them to hydrate.

🐾 Litter boxes should be cleaned daily. You should completely change the litter out from the litter box every two to four weeks depending on how many cats you have.

🐾 **Annual wellness:** Your cat's happiness and well-being are dependent on keeping them healthy. You should always take your cat to receive an annual wellness exam. Early detection and preventive care are important and can save your cat's life.

LOVE

Above all, your cat needs love. Make time every day to play with, love, and be with your cat.

ABOUT THE AUTHOR

Nala Cat holds the Guinness World Record for being the most popular cat on Instagram. She has a loyal fan base with well over six million followers. Nala has partnered with brands such as Google, Lyft, FreshStep, and L.O.L. Toys. And she has appeared in *People*, *USA Today*, *Forbes*, and more. A former shelter cat, Nala is known for her large, adorable eyes and charming demeanor. This is Nala's literary debut.

**YOU CAN FIND NALA
@NALA_CAT
SPREADING HAPPINESS AND LOVE.**